PURPOSEFUL PATHWAYS

LIFE LESSONS FOR MOVING FORWARD

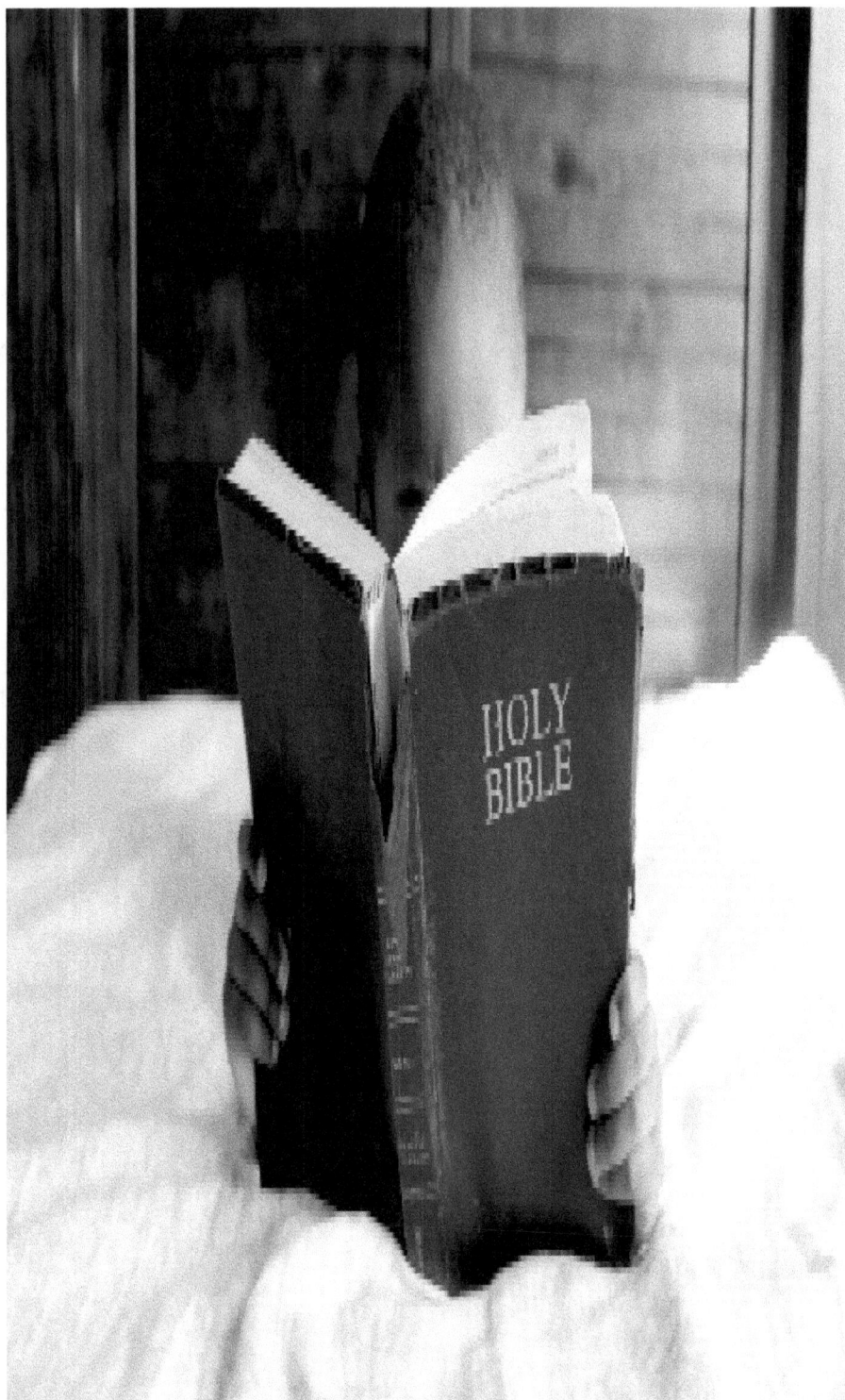

Purposeful Pathways

Life Lessons for Moving Forward

Purposeful Pathways

Life Lessons for Moving Forward

Dr. Sharon E. Flowers

Designed By - Adrishi Yadava.

ISBN13 : 9781947656635

Dedication

I dedicate this book to my Lord and Savior, Jesus Christ. Without Him, I am not anything, but with Him, I am everything! To my Mother, Father, and Grandmother, I love you all! To all of my children, you have blessed me beyond measure! To my Husband, Nathaniel, thank you for continuing to inspire, to encourage, and to love me beyond what sometimes may feel is impossible!

"Speak Life:

You are loved.

You have purpose.

You are a masterpiece.

You are wonderfully made.

God has a great plan for you."

-Germany Kent

Table of Contents

Acknowledgments

The completion of this book would not be at all possible without the assistance and encouragement of so many people whose names may not all be enumerated. Their contributions have inspired, and I am forever indebted. However, there are a few people I want to express my deepest appreciation:

My dearest Husband, Nathaniel A. Flowers thank you for sharing this rollercoaster ride with me! You have stood with me during the toughest of times, and loved beyond my pain! Thank you! Gladys McCray, Johnnie L. McCray Sr., Charlene Lewis, Jennifer Chairs, Johnnie L. McCray Jr., Terry Williams, Sharon Cannady, Wanda Boulton, Jackie Coaxum, Karina Broussard, Pastor Robert Cale, Donte Thomas, Hope Hodges-Crumbley, Erika Rodgers-Underwood, Angela McCorkle, Corita Cooper, Debbie Forbes, Ramona Perry, Chrissy Lewis and Sabrina Bentley-Thompson thank you all for cheering me to the finish line!

My dear friends Herbert and Toni Geddis, there is so much I can say, but thanks for walking this journey with me….30 years is long time and I can't wait to see what the next 30 has in store for us! To my 226/229th Family, I have nothing but LOVE for you all! Thank you for help shaping me into the woman I am today! To all of my military Brothers and Sisters too many to name, but thank you for all you have done for my family… you know who you are!

To Vicki Craig and all of my Children, thank you for making this leg of the journey sweeter and more fruitful; *it is sweeter* than I could have ever imagined! Special thanks to Bobby and my Grandma Irene for teaching us all how to love beyond limits! Thanks to Wyvetta Granger for being an Amazing leader and Woman of God!

To all of my relatives, my Sisters and friends who have supported me over the years! To Pastor Leo and Norma Davis (Love Alive Church), thank you for helping me find my purpose and ushering me back to my Purposeful Pathway!

To Iris and the Butterfly Typeface Publishing, thank you for helping this vision come to pass! Your leadership, vision, and passion has Blessed me beyond measure! I am more Blessed because of You!

To My Lord and Savior the visionary, the author of all knowledge and wisdom; thank you for your love and grace!

Foreword

Purposeful Pathways is a reminder to us to trust God even when there seems to be no silver lining. Author, Dr. Sharon Flowers is on a mission to help people see the light, in the midst of their darkness. She creates a clear view of God's faithfulness and His ability to do all things exceedingly and abundantly above all. In this book, she shows us that even when we're going through harsh seasons, the "winter" season, that God is equipping us with the tools we need to tackle this thing called life. When dealing with the death of a loved one, divorce or even thoughts of suicide, it's easy to get sucked into depression and lose faith. It's easy to lose sight of God's love and His plans for us. Purposeful Pathways is full of true events of people who go through pain and adversity, but they eventually allow God to take them through the healing process.

Dr. Flowers, who is no stranger to trauma and pain herself, takes us on a God-led journey to show us that trusting God and surrendering to His will is an imperative step to living whole and healthy lives. Purposeful Pathways teaches us that, even in the midst of turmoil, when we're experiencing a harsh season where things may be cold, dead and dried up, that in God, our roots, like withered trees, are still intact and God is continuously working for our good.

Lady Wyvetta Granger

First Lady Of New Life Community Church

Introduction

My interest in the mind and how it works (Psychology) developed from a need to understand what was going on with me mentally.

At a very young age, I endured sexual trauma. Later, I suffered combat trauma during my military service, and in 2012, my late husband, Bobby L. Boose, was murdered in Fayetteville, NC.

These jarring disturbances not only left physical scars, but emotional ones as well. As a result, I developed some self-destructive behaviors.

I struggled with alcoholism and even tried to commit suicide on several occasions, but God had much more in store for my life.

In September of 1999, I was saved at the age of 30.

As I grew in my faith, I began to cultivate an interest in applying Christian principles with psychology.

God, in His infinite wisdom, allowed me to endure the hurt, pain, and loss I endured and yet hold on to His unchanging hands! He equipped me with *life lessons* to assist those who like me, have suffered what once appeared to be unsurmountable tragedies and circumstances, *to move forward*.

This book, along with mentoring, is my way of reaching back and helping young women and others by sharing ways of incorporating Christian principles with post traumatic growth in the aftermath of trauma.

A Journey

As small child I use to dream about what my life would be like as an adult. I dreamed of living in a nice house, having food in the refrigerator, having lights, and having water. It may sound trivial to some, but I knew I didn't want to experience hunger pains or to eat ketchup sandwiches again because there was no food. I didn't want to experience the lights or water being shut off because my Mom couldn't afford to pay the bill. My Mother was a single parent struggling to take care of four young children, and money was tight. I didn't really realize, until I was about 18-years-old, that this was the start of my journey. I was always thinking about how I was going to go to college or get a job. I was creating a plan of action, and I was determined not to allow anything to stop me from accomplishing my dream.

My journey started with me joining the Army, and of course, this was only supposed to be a four year commitment so I could get the Montgomery GI Bill. My plan was to attend college at night while serving, but this was delayed due to my first deployment to Desert Shield/Storm, and so I reenlisted for four more years. During this time, my husband at the time had an affair, and I went through a horrible divorce. This situation caused me some financial and mental strain, and so I reenlisted for four more years. Even though I had encountered some rough situations along this journey, I was still finding the time to take some classes.

At one point in the journey, I was put in a mental ward for a few days; however, I consider this my timeout! It was God's way of getting my attention…it was a road bump in my journey. Nevertheless, this situation was not intended to stop me but to give me the wakeup call needed to get back on the right path! I eventually finished my associate's degree and continued on towards my bachelor's. By this time, I had almost 10 years in the Army and was progressing quite well. I really had never considered making the Army a career (God's plan), so I reenlisted indefinitely! I was promoted to Staff Sergeant, and things were looking great! I stayed in the Army 20 years and achieved the rank of Master Sergeant prior to retiring. I was able to complete my bachelor's and master's degrees before retiring. I will not say there weren't difficult days, but with God, all things are possible!

A journey is an act or instance of traveling from one place to another or our course of life on earth. What do you do before you start a journey?

1. You research the distance if you are driving, and the time it takes to get there. If you are going to school, you have your plan of study which details all of your classes, how many you should take each semester, and the timeframe in which you should be complete.

2. We know that during the journey we must consider the extra time to stop for the restroom breaks, eating, and stretching. We plan for unplanned interruptions and go back to make adjustments.

3. In considering the breaks, it may add some time, but we don't quit! We keep going because we have allotted for this in our planning.

I wanted to use this analogy to compare to our lives! Our life is a journey with some stops, curves, bends, and long straight ways along the way! I had quite a few interruptions, but this was only for me to catch my breath to get ready for the next step in the journey! The interruption or distraction doesn't mean we should QUIT, it means we do what is necessary along the stop and continue the journey!

Jeremiah 29:10-11 (MSG)

10-11 This is God's Word on the subject: "As soon as Babylon's seventy years are up and not a day before, I'll show up and take care of you as I promised and bring you back home. I know what I'm doing. I have it all planned out—plans to take care of you, not abandon you, plans to give you the future you hope for."

Life Lesson #1

Start Your Journey

The Angel Encounter

I had been assigned to my Army installation in Korea for almost three weeks, and things seemed to be going well. I enjoyed my job so far, and I had met some great people. My heart and mind seemed to be playing tug of war; my heart was saying, "Here is your new beginning; embrace it."

My mind was saying, "This is only temporary, and if you don't ever want to feel the hurt again, stick to the plan." I had gotten into some trouble at my last military assignment, but God allowed me to leave that assignment without any repercussions. I am not sure why I even cared what happened at that point; my life was out of control, and my husband at the time had just fathered a child with another woman. This was such heartbreak for a young lady in her mid-twenties, still searching for an unconditional love.

During those three weeks in Korea, I had learned how to commute to the different camps by the military bus systems, but of course, my adventurous side did not want to be limited. The military bus system stopped running at 10 pm on weekdays and at 1 am on weekends which was hardly enough time to explore the local communities. We had some local Koreans who worked on our military base, and I had gotten maps from the train and bus stations. They explained what each of the colors symbolized on the train maps and which bus would take me directly to Seoul. They made sure I knew which bus numbers would always drop me off directly in front of the gate of our base. I figured, since I was here, I might as well enjoy a little of South Korea and learn some of the history.

After being there a little over a month, I decided the time had come for what I had planned and the real reason I wanted to come to Korea. I had been contemplating committing suicide and had been planning this for some time. The day has finally gotten here. I seemed enthusiastic about what I was getting ready to do, but my mind seemed to keep wondering back to those who I knew loved me. The thoughts of how they would feel and think were bombarding my mind. I hadn't really considered all of my options, but somehow this seemed easier.

I went to my room to take my own life, but before I did this act, I decided to lie down in the bed. As I laid there, I thought I might have drifted off into a sleep, but not really. Anyway, I remember something (which I say was an angel) came and wrapped its arms around me so tightly.

I can still remember the love I felt, and the words the angel whispered, "Everything will be all right, and I love you!"

All of a sudden it was gone...I remember jumping up and looking around that tiny room thinking what was that? I can tell you from that day on, I was all right, and suicide was no longer the plan. However, the plan became how to live! I called to tell my Grandmother about the experience, and she told me that she knew something was wrong with me. She said she asked God to dispatch an Angel to come and see about her granddaughter! He answered her prayer!

In Psalm 34:17-18 it states, "The righteous cry out, and the Lord hears them; he delivers them from all their trouble. The Lord is close to the brokenhearted and saves those who are crushed in spirit." (NIV)

What has you brokenhearted and crushed in your spirit? It is time to cry out to the Lord!

Life Lesson #2

Heal Your Broken Heart

Caught in the Middle

My daughter and I were riding to church one Sunday, and she began to explain to me a situation concerning her friend. Her friend was currently living with her Step-Mother and biological Father, and because of a huge disagreement with the biological mother, the child was ripped from her home. Ultimately, the child was blamed by the Father for planning with the biological Mother to create havoc to leave the home. The Father no longer would speak to the daughter which has caused her to suffer depression and feel isolated from her 4-year-old brother.

My daughter could not understand why these adults could not co-parent together for the sake of her friend. This story is birthed out from not only this situation, but our own unique family structure. God has a way of handling things that is so sweet, but we must allow Him to mend our broken hearts and set the captives free so that we can effectively nurture and raise children to become healthy adults.

I did not realize my 13-year-old daughter understood what co-parenting really meant, so I asked her. She told me she watched how her father, I, and Ms. Vicki co-parented her brothers. We had such a unique family structure. When I married my late husband, he had two children from a previous marriage and two children from his first marriage. The oldest two children lived with us, and the two youngest would visit during the summers and spring break. The oldest two kid's mother was

20

not actively involved in their lives, so there was not much we could do in this particular situation. Ms. Vicki entrusted her two sons to come into my home every chance they could, and I am not sure whether we sat down and had a conversation about putting them first or not. One thing I do know is all of the children had to come first, and it was about them.

The children should never be caught in the middle of our failures, our mistakes, our lack of understanding, or our lack of forgiveness! In 1 Peter 2:1(NLT) it states, "So get rid of all evil behavior. Be done with all deceit, hypocrisy, jealousy, and all unkind speech." When we decided to leave the previous relationship by divorce, and there are children involved, there is a responsibility to have a conversation about forgiveness and love. It is hard to move forward holding on to the past hurts! Philippians 3:13 (NLT) states, "No, dear brothers and sisters, I have not achieved it, but I focus on this one thing: Forgetting the past and looking forward to what lies ahead... Also consider this passage of scripture as well, "Make a clean break with all cutting, backbiting, profane talk. Be gentle with one another, sensitive. Forgive one another as quickly and thoroughly as God in Christ forgave you." (Eph 4:31-32) (MSG) None of us are perfect, but there is One who is, and His name is Jesus! He is able to heal us all, but we must let go of pride or how we personally feel about the situation! After all, He is a God of Second Chances!

My late husband has gone home to be with the Lord, but Ms. Vicki and I understood that we still needed to co-parent! Our children have become responsible adults and are flourishing! I love Ms. Vicki like a sister, and I know that I can entrust my daughter to her. My daughter recently went to visit her brothers, but she stayed with Ms. Vicki...I count it a sheer blessing and joy that I am able to still co-parent with her! I am my Sister's Keeper!

What keeps you from effectively co-parenting? What are you doing to change your actions concerning the situation? Remember you are LOVED!

Life Lesson #3

Your Compromises

Financial Whirlpool

When you mention the word finances or money to most people, they would rather cover up their ears or bury their heads in sand. I know that I used to be one of those people and thank God that I can laugh about it now! I used to be the emoji monkey, the one with his eyes covered…LOL! This is especially true for most Christians as we have not governed our finances according to the Bible. Many of us feel like we are in a whirlpool, and it is not going to stop spinning. A whirlpool is defined as a rapidly rotating mass of water in a river or sea into which objects may be drawn, typically caused by the meeting of conflicting currents. Our debt is exceeding our income, and it is causing us some conflicting currents. We are drowning in debt, and society tells us it is all right to have credit. Society never speaks of the responsibility of using credit, but only what you can have.

I have heard so many say I have been blessed with a new car, house, and etc. If you are struggling to pay for it, to pay for the insurance, to pay for the maintenance on the car and property…it is not a blessing! In Proverbs 10:22 (AMP) it states, "The blessing of the Lord brings [true] riches,"

"And He adds no sorrow to it [for it comes as a blessing from God]." Simply put, you will not struggle to pay for anything when it comes from God!

When we are in debt, we are in bondage, and in Proverbs 22:7 (MSG) it states, "The poor are always ruled over by the rich, so don't borrow and put yourself under their power." God wants people to be blessed beyond measure, but we must listen and take heed to His Word! Proverbs 13:18 (MSG) states, "Refuse discipline and end up homeless; embrace correction and live an honored life." This does not mean we should not finance a car or a house or those credit cards! The average American household debt is $5,700, and the average for balance-carrying households is $16,048. In some cases, this is half our yearly salary! It is time for us to get out of this financial whirlpool and be better stewards over what God has blessed us with!

Do you think it is time that we reevaluate how we see and think about our finances?

There are some things we are supposed to be doing, but because our finances are in a whirlpool creating some conflicting currents, we believe that we can't. We should be creating wealth for future generations, and in Proverbs 13:22 it states, "A good man leaves an inheritance to his children's children, and the wealth of the sinner is stored up for [the hands of] the righteous."

Someone asked, "How are we supposed to leave an inheritance for future generations?" There are 3 fundamental principles to creating wealth, and they sound fairly easy but may seem hard to do to some.

1. Save/Invest

We are supposed to be saving and investing some money according to God's Word. In Matt 27:14-27 (MSG) it states, "It's also like a man going off on an extended trip. He called his servants together and delegated responsibilities. To one he gave five thousand dollars, to another two thousand, to a third one thousand, depending on their abilities. Then he left. Right off, the first servant went to work and doubled his master's investment. The second did the same. But the man with the single thousand dug a hole and carefully buried his master's money. After a long absence, the master of those three servants came back and settled up with them. The one given five thousand dollars showed him how he had doubled his investment. His master commended him: 'Good work! You did your job well. From now on be my partner.' The servant with the two thousand showed how he also had doubled his master's investment. His master commended him: 'Good work! You did your job well. From now on be my partner.' The servant given one thousand said, 'Master, I know you have high standards and hate careless ways, that you demand the best and make no allowances for error. I was afraid I might disappoint you, so I found a good hiding place and secured your money. Here it is, safe and sound down to the last cent.' The master was furious. 'That's a terrible way to live! It's criminal to live cautiously like that! If you knew I was after the best, why did you do less than the least? The least you could have done would have been to invest the sum with the bankers, where at least I would have gotten a little interest.'"

2. Give

Many people do not like to give, but my Grandmother used to say, "How can you receive anything if your hand is always closed?" She used say, "Don't be stingy with what you have, but share it with others. If you open your hand to others, you can be ready to receive as well."

What a great analogy! In 2 Corinthians 9:7 (MSG) it states, "I want each of you to take plenty of time to think it over and make up your own mind what you will give. That will protect you against sob stories and arm-twisting. God loves it when the giver delights in the giving."

Proverbs 11:25 (MSG) states, "The one who blesses others is abundantly blessed; those who help others are helped."

Luke 6:38 (MSG) states, "Give away your life; you'll find life given back, but not merely given back — given back with bonus and blessing. Giving, not getting, is the way. Generosity begets generosity."

Proverbs 11:25 (MSG) states, "The one who blesses others is abundantly blessed; those who help others are helped."

3. Spend some

God requires us to be good stewards with everything He blesses us with! Don't be wasteful and buy things you don't need. It is all right to still use coupons, shop in the clearance section, and not buy name brand clothes! Isaiah 55:2 (MSG) states, "Why do you spend your money on junk food, your hard-earned cash on cotton candy? Listen to me, listen well: Eat only the best, fill yourself with only the finest. Pay attention, come close now, listen carefully to my life-giving, life-nourishing words." Now this doesn't mean not to buy your children any cotton candy or donuts at the County Fair; but you would not use your whole paycheck to buy these items.

It would be wasteful and not healthy for our children.

Are you tired of the financial whirlpool? Well, it is time to stop spinning and learn to do it God's way! Seek the help of a financial advisor! You are LOVED!

Life Lesson #4

Your Financial Status

Forgiveness

This is a topic I guess many struggle with, including myself. Many have asked, "Can you truly forgive someone?"

The answer is yes! I already know there is someone reading this who is very skeptical right now, but I want you to keep reading. God is definitely about to show you His unconditional love and the power of healing! I hope that you are blessed as I share my stories of hurt, pain, anger, and resentment but most importantly the road to being healed.

As a child, you expect the adults in your life to protect you from harm, especially when they say, "If anyone tries to touch you inappropriately you tell us."

What happens when it is a family member who sexually violates you? As a young child, it was not easy to tell my mother or any other family member what was happening to us. It wasn't only happening to me but to my cousins as well by the same Uncle. I already knew that if I told it would hurt my Mom deeply, and my other Uncles would possibly harm him in some way. I didn't want my other Uncles to end up in jail, and I did not want my Mom to experience any pain for feeling like she was unable to protect me. I decided that I would not tell, and eventually, Mom moved us away from there.

I hadn't thought about that ordeal for many years until one day when I received a phone call that he passed away. There were no tears; I only felt anger, resentment, and pain that I didn't get a chance to confront him. I did not attend his funeral, but I remember the wave of emotions towards him turned into hate. I had not forgiven him, and at this point, I did not want to. I had buried this ordeal many years ago, and I felt that he had molested me again with his death. I wanted to move pass this, but somehow, I could not just hide it away deep inside my heart this time.

I began to study forgiveness in the Bible, and I read this passage of scripture in Matthew 5:23-24 (MSG) "This is how I want you to conduct yourself in these matters. If you enter your place of worship and, about to make an offering, you suddenly remember a grudge a friend has against you, abandon your offering, leave immediately, go to this friend and make things right. Then and only then, come back and work things out with God."

In my case, it was my Uncle who had violated me and was now deceased. How was I going to make things right? I want you all to understand that it was not about my Uncle, but about me being free from the hurt, pain, anger, hatred, unforgiveness, and resentment. So, God told me to write him a letter expressing what his actions had done to me, but also how I chose to forgive him. I took this letter, dug a hole in a field, and buried the letter. For me, the burial of this letter was a translation of, "This thing no longer has any power over me! It is dead! I can now move on to freely worship God!" What or who in your life are you struggling to forgive?

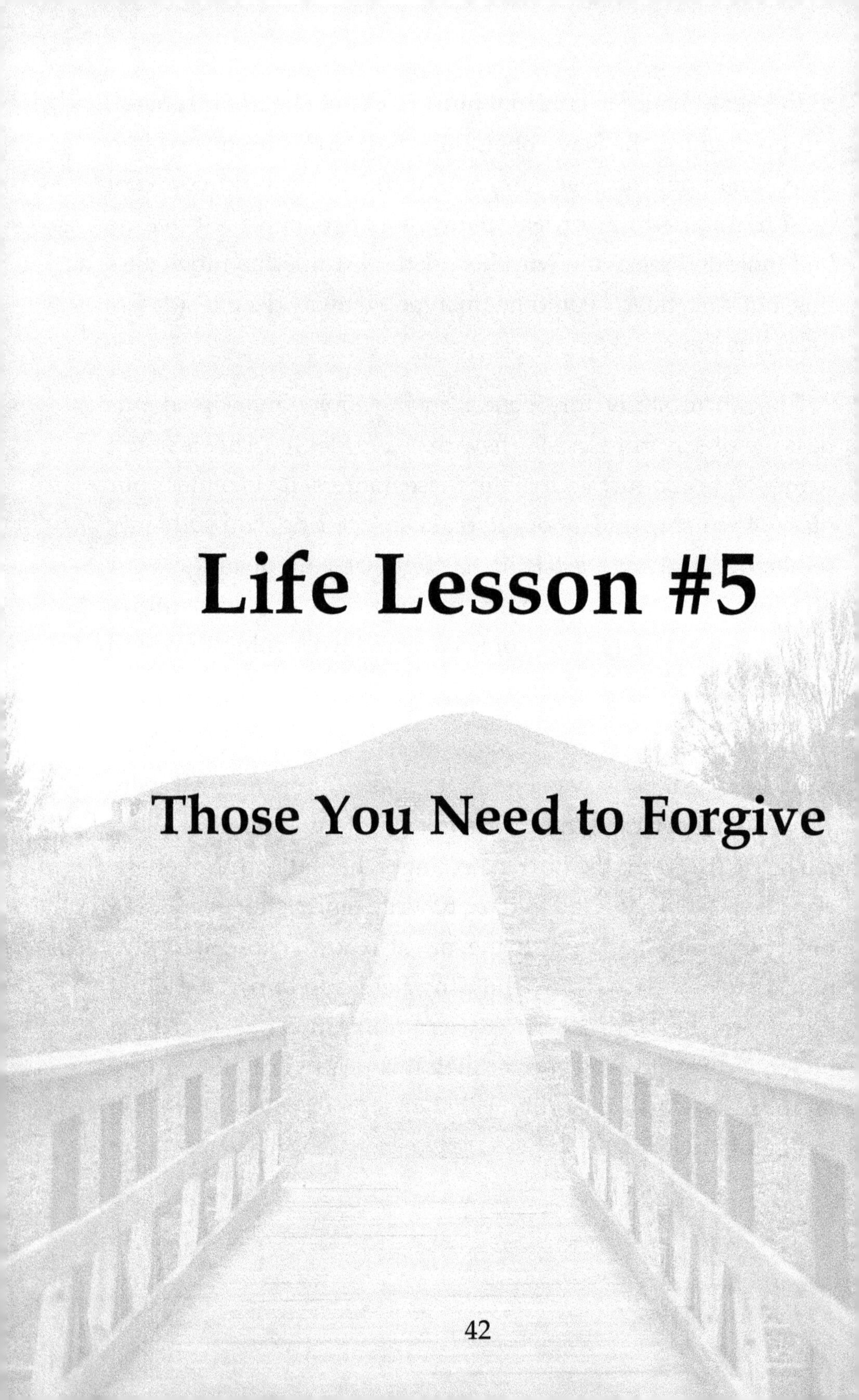

Life Lesson #5

Those You Need to Forgive

Forsaken, but not Forgotten

Has there ever been a time in your life where you allowed the enemy to convince you that all the suffering and pain was not worth struggle in which you were going through at the moment? I allowed satan to convince me that I was tired and didn't have the strength the keep fighting. Even though I was raised in the church and had a relationship with God, somewhere along the journey I renounced my position with the Lord. I gave up my walk with Christ, and the lifestyle in which I was living was no secret. When God has a plan for your life, no one or nothing can change this plan. I allowed my emotional state to override the voice of God! I could no longer hear God, but just satan feeding me his negative thinking. In Jos 1:8 (AMP) it states, "This Book of the Law shall not depart from your mouth, but you shall read [and meditate on] it day and night, so that you may be careful to do [everything] in accordance with all that is written in it; for then you will make your way prosperous, and then you will be successful." How could I be successful when I had renounced my position?

I thought about Rahab who was out of position with God, but recognized who God was in her sinful state. She still saw God's power working and had a reverence for God! Rahab hid the spies from the King and saved her whole household (Joshua 2). (KJV) Rahab, the harlot, became the wife of Salmon, who gave birth to Boaz. Boaz was the father of Obed, and Obed was the father of Jesse. Jesse was the father of David, and David becomes the forefather of Joseph. Joseph marries Mary who is the mother of Jesus…what an awesome and amazing God we serve that Rahab was not forgotten and she is in the lineage of our Savior!

Sure, there are situations that come to hinder God's plan, but it cannot change what God has ordained. I must remember I am in the Savior's lineage; I am in His family!

The word _forsakes_ means to give up; _renounce_; to leave altogether; abandon. We must remember God never leaves us; we leave him. Hebrews 13:5 (KJV), "…I will never leave thee, nor forsake thee."

The word _renounces_ means to reject; to disown; to give up by formal announcement. When we decide that we have had enough of God, we do not make the formal announcement with words, but it is in our lifestyle.

The word _forgotten_ means to lack concern for; neglect. When we don't pray or read our Bibles like we should, it is a lack of concern and could be seen as we have forgotten about God. But a still small voice comes to remind you that He loves you and has not forgotten about you!

Life Lesson #6

Your Forgotten Concerns

Getting Past the Coal to See the Diamond in You!

Have you ever looked in a mirror and thought you just didn't like what you saw? I don't know too many women who haven't, especially when we try to define ourselves by what society considers beautiful.

In Psalms 139:14 (KJV), it says, "I will praise thee; for I am fearfully and wonderfully made: marvelous are thy works; and that my soul knoweth right well."

Somewhere along the way, we have forgotten that we are fearfully and wonderfully made, and God's creations are marvelous. What is going on in the inside of us that we can't see ourselves how God sees us? Many of us think the transformation starts on the outside, but it starts on the inside. Romans 12:2 (NLT) says, "Don't copy the behavior and customs of this world, but let God transform you into a new person by changing the way you think."

**Transforms** means to change something completely and usually in a good way; to change in character or condition.

When we think about coal, it is usually dark and dirty, but coal is a black or brownish-black solid combustible substance formed by the partial decomposition of vegetable matter without free access to air. We decompose when we abuse our body, and neglect our God-given gifts. Why are we decomposing when we have the ability to choose life or death? We have free access to the Word of God which is life changing and transforming. It is all in how we think, how we define ourselves! I am not defined by what society says I should be or look like but, what God says I am. So, how does transformation happen? I am so glad you asked.

Transformation is a process, and it doesn't all happen at once. We are being "transformed" into His likeness; so, we spend a lifetime learning how to live the new life we have in Christ. Our minds can be a constant battleground, and we must continually bring every negative thought captive to God's Word. In 2 Corinthian 10:3-6 (MSG) it states, "The world is unprincipled. It's dog-eat-dog out there! The world doesn't fight fair. But we don't live or fight our battles that way—never have and never will. The tools of our trade aren't for marketing or manipulation, but they are for demolishing that entire massively corrupt culture. We use our powerful God-tools for smashing warped philosophies, tearing down barriers erected against the truth of God, fitting every loose thought, emotion, and impulse into the structure of life shaped by Christ. Our tools are ready at hand for clearing the ground of every obstruction and building lives of obedience into maturity." Please understand the change in our spirit comes about immediately, but it can take a little while for the change to be reflected in our soul and flesh!

We must continually seek God and know that this transformation is not something we can do on our own. We must unite with the Creator, and we do this by continuing to allow God to work in our lives; however, we must work as well.

In Philippians 2:12-13 (MSG) it states, "What I'm getting at, friends, is that you should simply keep on doing what you've done from the beginning. When I was living among you, you lived in responsive obedience. Now that I'm separated from you, keep it up. Better yet, redouble your efforts. Be energetic in your life of salvation, reverent and sensitive before God. That energy is God's energy, an energy deep within you. God, Himself, is willing and is working at what will give Him the most pleasure."

What is our part in laboring with God?

1. Believe in His Word. (Hew 11:1, 11:6)
2. Choose! (Deut 30:19-20)
3. Focus on God's Divine wisdom of the Word of God. (Col 3:16) (2Tim 3:16) (John 17:17)
4. Keep your mind focused on good things (Guard your thoughts). (Phil 4:8)
5. Pray without ceasing. (James 1:5. 4:2, 5:16, Matt 7:7)
6. Persevere; Don't give up! (Luke 18:1, Heb 6:11, Matt 11:12)
7. Resist the enemy! (James 4:7, Rom 7:23, Gal 5:17)
8. Do not forget the vision. (Prov 29:18, Hab 2:2)

A diamond is a native crystalline carbon that is the hardest known mineral. It is usually nearly colorless. When transparent and free from flaws, it is highly valued as a precious stone.

The difference between us and an actual diamond is God already sees us as precious with all of our flaws, and in His eyes, we are valuable! What is stopping you from getting past the coal to see the diamond in you?

Life Lesson #7

Your Renewed Mind

_____

_____

_____

_____

_____

_____

_____

_____

_____

_____

_____

_____

_____

_____

Grieve It Out

I had been happily married to my best friend for almost 11 years, and life was going great! We both retired from the military and had started new careers. Our oldest four children were either in the military or college; so, we just had our baby girl, Gabriela, home with us. At this time, she was 7-years-old and the apple of her Daddy's eye! Bobby spent a lot of time with her, and she loved being with her Dad. We had spent the last year traveling. It almost seemed as if we were making up for lost time. Bobby seemed to be on a mission, and he was getting all he could done to fulfill the promises he had made.

On November 2, 2012, my life was turned upside down and inside out. Bobby was kidnapped and murdered. The week prior, I had attended a Bible study in which the topic was on "Seasons." Each of us was asked to describe which season of our lives we were experiencing, and I said winter. I really didn't understand why I said winter because everything was going great! As I sat there listening, the Lord spoke to me and said, "Look outside at the tree right outside the window." The tree did not have any leaves and looked wilted. When you looked at the trunk of the tree, its roots were strong and firmly planted. God said, "This is a reminder for you that in your winter season that you may look barren and wilted, but just as the tree is firmly planted so are you!"

The night I was notified of Bobby's death, I can't say I remembered what God said to me about my winter season. The word *grief* is a small five letter word that can wreak havoc in a person's life. The pain of the loss of something or someone can leave you feeling overwhelmed. Bobby's loss was one of the biggest challenges that I have had to face. I experienced shock, anger, disbelief, guilt, and profound sadness. I was unable to eat, sleep, or even think straight at times. Oh yes, these are all normal reactions initially! I remember asking God how long the hole would stay in my heart? I told the Lord that if I have to wake up every morning with this aching and feeling of emptiness, I was not going to make it. I needed Him to help me "Grieve it Out"!

What does that mean? I had to acknowledge that I was in pain and deeply hurt by his loss. I had to accept that I would have some unexpected emotions and feelings concerning Bobby's death. I had to learn that even when I had these unexpected emotions and feelings, it didn't mean I had not forgiven the people who had taken his life! I had to learn to accept the support from the people whom God placed in my life. I had to learn how to take care of myself physically and emotionally (Yes, I sought counseling). I could not be a mother to my children if I was not whole and healthy!

I prayed for the people who took his life and their families! In my prayer time, God allowed me to remember what He told me about my winter season. It encouraged me to continue my process to "Grieve it Out." I accepted my new journey and my new path! I began to volunteer at my daughter's school and at the church's food pantry. Also, I would speak to other widows encouraging them to embrace their new journey but not to rush it! Everyone is different, and the grief process is unique to each of us. Bobby had told me that if he died before me, he did not want me just to exist but to live. In my journey of life, God sent a dear friend that I had known for 20 years to be a blessing in my life. I didn't know that God had a greater plan, and 2 years after Bobby went to be with the Lord, we got married! God's way to "Grieve it Out" is better than any plan I have seen yet!

Life Lesson #8

Your Grieves

His Amazing Love

As I sit here and reflect on God's amazing love, I often find it hard to comprehend its true depths. In John 3:16 (TLB), it states, "For God loved the world so much that he gave his only Son so that anyone who believes in him shall not perish but have eternal life." I can honestly say that I am not sure if I could give up my precious children for anyone, but that is the true kind of love that God has for all of us! God sees things afar off, and He knew exactly the path of my life. It is no surprise to Him the hurts, disappoints, the joys, and the pains I would experience. But His amazing love guides, and it provides us what is necessary. It brings wholeness and completes us in ways that are indescribable in mere words! So, this is how my story starts with God using these people in my life to help me see that He was always with me, but even more importantly, He showed me how love can heal the brokenhearted and set the captive free.

It initially started one morning as I was preparing to head to the courthouse, and I was waiting on my cousin to pick me up. Of course, as she entered the house with her sassy and bold self, she began to say that God had given her something to tell me. She knew that I would not immediately be receptive to what she was saying, because it had only been a few months since the passing of Bobby. She told me that I would not be a widow for long and that I would remarry sooner than what I thought. She was right; I was mad. I could not believe she had the audacity to walk up in my house to say those words. After she spoke, she said, "Let's go; we need to go take care of all this paperwork." I don't recall if we ever really spoke about what she said that day. To be honest, I didn't care if we did. I was so consumed by my anger. and I missed that God had spoken.

My daughter, Gabby, who was 8-years-old at the time, did not seem to miss a beat after her father's passing. I remember walking through the house one day, and she asked, "Mom, are you still sad about Daddy?"

I said, "Yes."

Her response was, "I don't know why…. he is Heaven with Jesus!"

I guess that meant snap out of it! We had taught her the Word of God, and she was only giving the love I needed. I can't say I really heard her that day, but it was beginning to sink in. One morning on the way to school, she began to tell me that it was okay for me to get married again. I asked her who I would marry. She said she did not know, but her Godfather seemed like a nice man. I told her that Daddy loves us very much and that she would always have a father.

Gabby's response was, "Mom, I know that Daddy loves me, but he is in Heaven. I need a Dad here who I can touch and feel every day." Out of the mouth of babes…Yes, the Lord spoke, and He had my full attention.

On January 24, 2014, my dear friend Nathaniel Flowers was visiting Fayetteville, and he would always come see us. I took him to lunch to celebrate his retirement, but nothing unusual happened between us. I had tickets for an upcoming Tyler Perry play and was wondering if he would be interested in going if he was in the area. I remember having an awesome time, and it seemed as if we talked for a while. Nathaniel returned home, and we began to talk more than usual. I enjoyed the laughter; I could finally smile from my heart! It was a natural/pure transition, and I knew it was God! I did not doubt his love for us, and I knew he was willing to do what was needed for us to become a family! He changed his retirement plans and relocated to North Carolina. Nathaniel accepted me for who I was…despite all of the issues I currently had going on in my life. He stood with me during the trials and has been a phenomenal Father to Gabby! She has flourished and continues to be an honor roll student! In my wildest dreams, I never thought that I could experience true love again; I was so wrong! I have this amazing man/Husband, who God has ordained for this journey of my life, and He knew exactly what I needed! HIS Love transcends! IT WAS HIS PLAN!

Life Lesson #9

The Life God Has for You

The Miracle Worker

A couple of days ago, I was in the shower, and I began to thank God for how good He has been to me over the years! It wasn't anything special that had happened that morning, but I was just grateful for life! In reflecting back over the years, I thought about some things that had left me physically and mentally scared, but God's grace and His healing power touched me on more than one occasion! I want to share this story with you about my early encounter with sex, and how it left me physically unable to conceive. My first encounter was when I was about 12-years-old with a man who was 19-years-old. Naive about sexual intercourse and the other female issues, I was physically unable to conceive a baby. Due to these issues, satan used this physical issue as a sport on my emotions to tell me I was not a woman. I believed and convinced myself that I would not make a good mother, so I decided that I never wanted children. This was a way of protecting my heart, but in the inside, I felt hurt. I carried the burden that my ex-husband had been unfaithful and fathered a child with someone. All of this had taken a toll on me mentally and left wounds that needed to be healed. I never shared this with anyone until I married in 2001.

Prior to getting married, I shared with my husband that I was unable to conceive children. He also shared that he had a vasectomy but wanted to get a reversal. Due to my diagnosis, I did not want him to proceed with this procedure. He did not share with me that he proceeded with the paperwork to get the reversal completed, and drove himself to California to have the procedure done.

I found out after the procedure was completed, and he said, "God is still a Miracle Worker." He had the faith of a mustard seed, and I could too but only if I did not allow fear to keep me from trusting God! It took me two years to receive the promises of God, and on September 11, 2003, I found out that I was pregnant!! He is still the Miracle Worker! What miracle do you need God to perform in your life? He is still the Miracle Worker!

2 Timothy 1:7 New King James Version (NKJV)

"For God has not given us a spirit of fear, but of power and of love and of a sound mind."

Mark 5:34 Message (MSG)

"Jesus said to her, 'Daughter, you took a risk of faith, and now you're healed and whole. Live well, live blessed! Be healed of your plague.'"

Matthew 17:20 Message (MSG)

'"Because you're not yet taking God seriously,' said Jesus. 'The simple truth is that if you had a mere kernel of faith, a poppy seed, say, you would tell this mountain, 'Move!' and it would move. There is nothing you wouldn't be able to tackle.'"

Psalms 77:14 King James Version (KJV)

"You are the God who performs miracles; you display your power among the peoples."

Life Lesson #10

God's Miracles and You!

_____

_____

_____

_____

_____

_____

_____

_____

_____

_____

_____

_____

_____

_____

Redeeming the Time

The word _**redeeming**_ means to compensate for a defect.

I want us to reflect back to when we were young, and we had dreams of becoming a doctor, lawyer, teacher, nurse, business owner, designer, etc. Some of us abandoned those dreams because we thought we were being selfish in pursuing what we thought was our dream and not God's plan for our life. In Jeremiah 29:11 (MSG) it states, "I know what I'm doing. I have it all planned out - plans to take care of you, not abandon you, plans to give you the future you hope for."

Maybe lately you have been feeling hopeless, and that it is too late to pursue your dream. When you wake up in morning with health and the fullness of life, it is not too late!! We all have a purpose to fulfill; so, what is the defect? It is the abandonment of the dream; it is the lie the enemy has whispered when he said, "It is too late."

It is the belief that it is selfish to pursue your purpose. How can it be selfish to pursue what God has placed in you?

You must pursue your dream...the word _**pursue**_ means to overtake and capture. I am reminded of the story of King David and his men in 1 Samuel 30:1-8 (NLT). These verses of how King David and those who went with him to battle returned home to Ziklag to find the Amalekites had destroyed their homes by burning them to the ground and had taken their wives/children. Can you imagine the hopelessness, despair, devastation, and pain he must have felt? Do you think maybe he felt it was too late to do anything about what had taken place? Maybe so? Especially when the men who had went with him were so angry, they thought of stoning him to death. King David did not stay in this place of despair, hopelessness, or devastation, but he found his strength in the Lord!

Only for a short time did King David have a defect in his thinking; so, he began to redeem the time. In 1 Samuel 30:7-8 (NLT), "David said to Abiathar the priest, 'Bring me the ephod!' So Abiathar brought it. Then David asked the Lord, 'Should I chase after this band of raiders? Will I catch them?'"

"And the Lord told him, 'Yes, go after them. *You will surely recover everything that was taken from you!*'" The Lord did not say you might or it is possible, but He said you will surely recover everything that was taken from you!

The time is now for you to pursue God's promises for you! Ephesians 5:16 (AMP) states, "[16] making the very most of your time [on earth, recognizing and taking advantage of each opportunity and using it with wisdom and diligence], because the days are [filled with] evil."

What dreams or purpose have yet to be fulfilled? How do you plan to fulfill them? Now that you have your written plan, "Write it on a billboard large and clear, so that anyone can read it at a glance and rush to tell the others. (Habakkuk 2:2) (TLB), it is time to execute them. You are LOVED!

Life Lesson #11

Your Dreams and Purpose

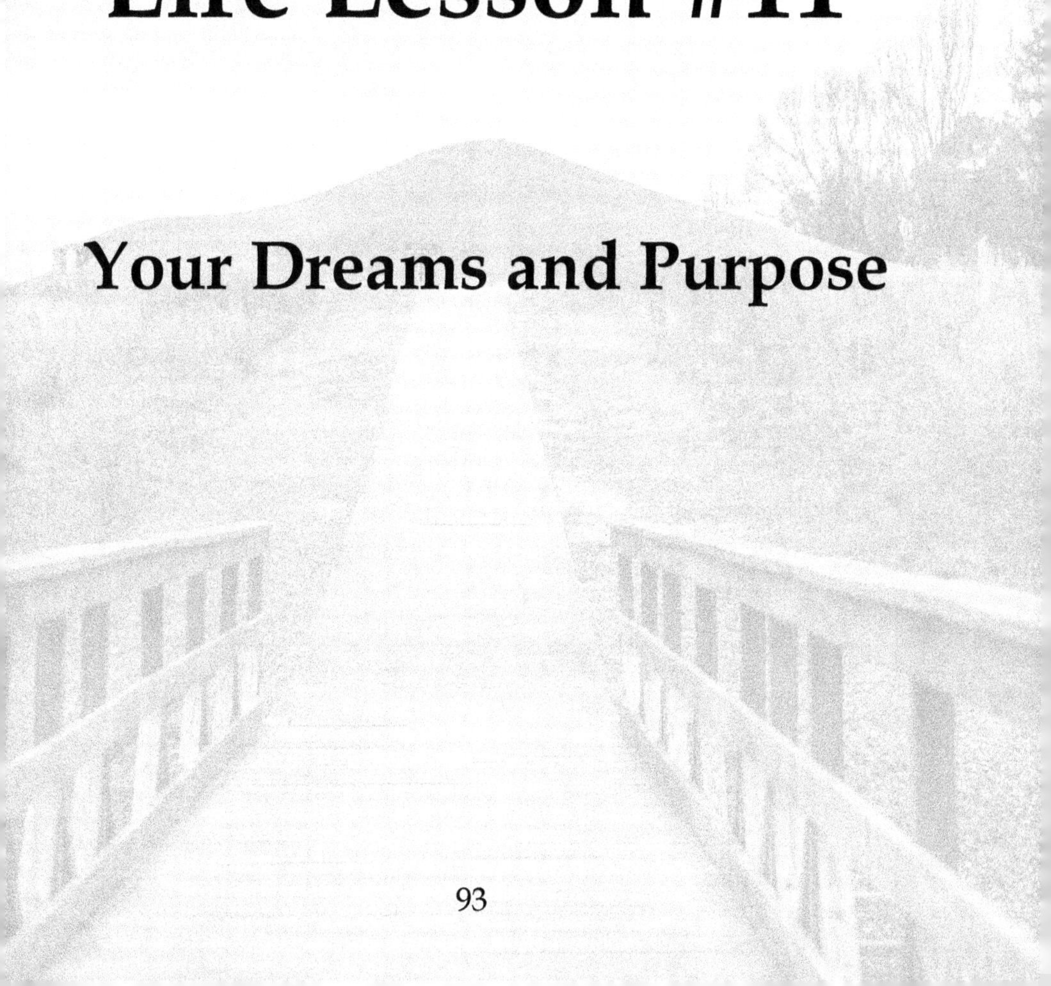

Reign Over Circumstances

On December 31, 2013, I remembered sitting in my house with all the lights out crying and asking God to help me! I felt so alone, helpless, misunderstood, and unloved. I knew part of this was a spiritual attack, and the other was me having a pity party! Yes, I had to admit that I wasn't the only one having a difficult time and that God had already given me the tools necessary to reign over my circumstances. I just hadn't used them.

As I began to reflect back over my life, I had been in some really rough situations and had some really bad things happen to me. I was sexually abused as a child, was locked up in a mental hospital, was in an abusive marriage, tried to commit suicide, suffered some Military Sexual Assault Trauma, and that was just the tip of the iceberg! I share these things because I want you to know that despite whatever you have gone through you can grow and move forward.

We all have a story, and we all have to walk out the journey that we call LIFE! God never meant for us to just stand still when we come to a fork in the road, but He wants us to seek Him and to choose to go left or right based on His guidance. God wants us to know that He has given us the power of prayer, praise, worship, and most importantly, His Word to *reign* over our circumstances! The word *reign* means to exercise authority or control (Merriam-Webster Online, 2017). I realized that I would no longer allow the circumstance to *reign* over me, but I will reign over it! I would reign over my circumstance through prayer (The Word of God), worship, faith, and LOVE!!

1 Corinthians 13:7-8 (AMP) states, "Love bears all things [regardless of what comes], believes all things [looking for the best in each one], hopes all things [remaining steadfast during difficult times], endures all things [without weakening]." "8 Love never fails [it never fades nor ends]."

I am so glad that I am not defined by my situation, and I am so glad this is not the end of my testimony. I am so glad that God said a mind that is kept in Christ would be kept in perfect peace [Isaiah 26:3] (AMP). "I can do all things through Christ which strengthens me." [Phil 4:13] (AMP) "Just as the body is dead without breath, so also faith is dead without good works." [James 2:26] (AMP) He said, "Sharon, you can't sit in self-pity, but you must get up and get to moving!"

I began to seek God as to what He wanted me to do, and I followed. I continued school and was able to finish my PhD. I moved into a new house and started my life as it was without my late husband. I volunteered at my daughter's school helping high schoolers prepare for college. I started back teaching part-time at a Bible College. In me serving God and doing what He told me, I began to grow and move forward! I was not focusing on what I had lost but what new path God laid before me. The blessings of God are yes and amen! This does not mean we won't experience any chaos in our lives...it means we must remember who the Chaos Fixer is! I am learning that whenever I am faced with a situation I need to evaluate it by the Word of

God! I am not defined by my situation, but I am victorious! I am victorious because of my faith in God! Over in Galatians 3:6-9: it states:

Galatians 3:6-9 New Living Translation (NLT)

"In the same way, Abraham believed God, and God counted him as righteous because of his faith. [7] The real children of Abraham, then, are those who put their faith in God."

"[8] What's more, the Scriptures looked forward to this time when God would declare the Gentiles to be righteous because of their faith. God proclaimed this good news to Abraham long ago when he said, 'All nations will be blessed through you.' [9] So all who put their faith in Christ share the same blessing Abraham received because of his faith." Remember Jesus has given us the tools to reign over our circumstances. The question is: Have you employed your tools?

Life Lesson #12

What Is Your Story?

_____

_____

_____

_____

_____

_____

_____

_____

_____

_____

_____

_____

_____

_____

_____

_____

_____

_____

_____

_____

_____

_____

_____

_____

_____

_____

_____

Relationships

I often hear so many women say they are waiting on their Boaz, or they will be so happy when they get married so they can have someone to take care of them. I often wonder why women want a man like Boaz? Is it because he was a mighty man of wealth? Or is it because he was a man of God? Do you ever wonder if there is something more you should be doing while you are waiting? Do we ever consider the relationship we have with God as we prepare for our earthly relationship? These questions are important as you really consider relationships and marriage.

1.Ruth understood loyalty, and valued her relationship with the Lord. After Naomi's husband and sons died, she urged Ruth to stay in her land with her family. Here is Ruth's response: Do not urge me to leave you or turn back from following you; for where you go, I will go, and where you lodge, I will lodge. Your people will be my people, and your God, my God. (Ruth 1:16 AMP) It was her love for God that compelled her in the decision she made. What is compelling you?

2. Ruth understood faith without taking action does not mean anything, and she understood God's Divine favor. Ruth was not seeking a husband, but she was seeking God's Favor! (Ruth 2:2-8) (AMP) And Ruth the Moabitess said to Naomi, "Please let me go to the field and glean among the ears of grain after one [of the reapers] in whose sight I may find favor." Naomi said to her, "Go, my daughter." [3] So Ruth went and picked up

the leftover grain in a field after the reapers; and she happened to stop at the plot of land belonging to Boaz, who was of the family of Elimelech. ⁴ It was then that Boaz came back from Bethlehem and said to the reapers, "The Lord be with you!" And they answered him, "The Lord bless you!" ⁵ Then Boaz said to his servant who was in charge of the reapers, "Whose young woman is this?" ⁶ The servant in charge of the reapers answered, "She is the young Moabite woman who came back with Naomi from the country of Moab. ⁷ And she said, 'Please let me glean and gather after the reapers among the [b]sheaves.' So she came and has continued [gathering grain] from early morning until now, except when she sat [resting] for a little while in the [field] house." ⁸ Then Boaz said to Ruth, "Listen carefully, my daughter. Do not go to glean in another field or leave this one, but stay here close by my maids. ⁹ Watch which field they reap, and follow behind them. I have commanded the servants not to touch you. And when you are thirsty, go to the [water] jars and drink from what the servants draw." Who or what are we seeking?

3. Ruth was kind and humble; this was her character! Ruth received favor from God and man!(Ruth 2:10-14) (AMP) ¹⁰ Then she kneeled face downward, bowing to the ground, and said to him, "Why have I found favor in your eyes that you should notice me, when I am a foreigner?" ¹¹ Boaz answered her, "I have been made fully aware of everything that you have done for your mother-in-law since the death of your husband, and how you have left your father and mother and the land of your birth, and have come to a people that you did not know before. ¹² May the Lord repay you for your kindness, and may your

reward be full from the Lord, the God of Israel, under whose wings you have come to take refuge." ¹³ Then she said, "Let me find favor in your sight, my lord, for you have comforted me and have spoken kindly to your maidservant, though I am not as one of your maidservants." ¹⁴ At mealtime Boaz said to her, "Come over here and eat some bread and dip your bread in the vinegar." So she sat beside the reapers; and he served her roasted grain, and she ate until she was satisfied and she had some left [for Naomi]. ¹⁵ When she got up to glean, Boaz ordered his servants, "Let her glean even among the sheaves, and do not insult her. ¹⁶ Also you shall purposely pull out for her some stalks [of grain] from the sheaves and leave them so that she may collect them, and do not rebuke her." Does your character align with character of Christ?

I am not saying there is anything wrong with desiring to be married, but are we desiring to married for the wrong reasons? If you continue to read the book of Ruth, you will find out that Naomi eventually asked Ruth where she had worked that day, and Naomi began to thank God that they had been redeemed. She already knew that Boaz was family and that he could marry Ruth. If you continue reading, he was not next in line to marry Ruth; however, the other family member gave up his opportunity and Boaz married Ruth. Remember our Father created us for relationship, and He has someone for you!! You are Loved!

Life Lesson #13

Your Aspirations

There's Always an Answer

I heard a message at church by Pastor Leo Davis, and title was "There's always an Answer," and this message began to stir my heart and mind. So, here I am to share with you a few words of encouragement! As I write this message of hope, I am inspired to take action. No longer will I sit silently by while satan wreaks havoc in people's lives. I am determined to offer them the hope that I have but also teach and demonstrate the principles as well. In the Bible, there is an answer for every situation, both naturally and spiritually. I want you to know today that Jesus loves you, and that it is never too late for change!

I have seen many write on Facebook about the desire for change in their lives, and they say how every time they take one step forward, it appears they are taking two steps backwards!

The word *appear* is an intransitive verb; which is characterized by not having or containing a direct object. The word *appear* in this sense means to have an outward aspect....*not really real.*

I want you to know there isn't anything intransitive about you! You are very real to God, and you are loved! God placed His love upon us by giving His Son as a sacrifice! John 3:16 (KJV) Yes, it was intentional; He gave up His Beloved Son for you and me!

God made the sacrifice for us to have life, so why are we not living? Some of us have allowed the enemy to make it *appear* that the dream is dead! It is not too late to fulfill the dreams the devil has been trying to steal or kill! Jesus is still the answer! Are you ready to take action? What area of your life do you need assistance?

Please read James 2:14-26 (MSG version)

Faith in Action

"[14-17] Dear friends, do you think you'll get anywhere in this if you learn all the right words but never do anything? Does merely talking about faith indicate that a person really has it? For instance, you come upon an old friend dressed in rags and half-starved and say, 'Good morning, friend! Be clothed in Christ! Be filled with the Holy Spirit!' and walk off without providing so much as a coat or a cup of soup—where does that get you? Isn't it obvious that God-talk without God-acts is outrageous nonsense?"

"[18] I can already hear one of you agreeing by saying, 'Sounds good. You take care of the faith department, I'll handle the works department.'"

"Not so fast. You can no more show me your works apart from your faith then I can show you my faith apart from my works. Faith and works, works and faith, fit together hand in glove."

"[19-20] Do I hear you professing to believe in the one and only God, but then observe you complacently sitting back as if you had done something wonderful? That's just great. Demons do that, but what good does it do them? Use your heads! Do you suppose for a minute that you can cut faith and works in two and not end up with a corpse on your hands?"

"21-24 Wasn't our ancestor Abraham 'made right with God by works' when he placed his son Isaac on the sacrificial altar? Isn't it obvious that faith and works are yoked partners, that faith expresses itself in works? That the works are 'works of faith?' The full meaning of 'believe' in the Scripture sentence, 'Abraham believed God and was set right with God,' includes his action. It's that mesh of believing and acting that got Abraham named 'God's friend.' Is it not evident that a person is made right with God not by a barren faith but by faith fruitful in works?"

"25-26 The same with Rahab, the Jericho harlot. Wasn't her action in hiding God's spies and helping them escape—that seamless unity of believing and doing—what counted with God? The very moment you separate body and spirit, you end up with a corpse. Separate faith and works and you get the same thing: a corpse."

Life Lesson #14

Your Faith

Questions for Thought & Discussion

1. Are you ready for change in your life? What prompted this desire?
2. Have you been on a journey? What are/were the details?
3. Do you know what it feels like to be broken? What were the circumstances? How did you handle it?
4. Have you had a supernatural or spiritual experience?
5. Are you good at compromise? Why or why not?
6. Do you believe your finances are connected to your emotional health?
7. Is it easy for you to forgive? Why or why not? What are the benefits of forgiving?
8. Do you neglect yourself? Do you neglect those you love? How?
9. What do you think about yourself? Are your thoughts the same as those around you?
10. Do you know how to grieve? Why is it important to grieve?
11. Do you know the love of God? How do you feel it?
12. Have you experienced a miracle? Do you know someone who has? What were the circumstances?
13. What are your life dreams and goals? Are you working toward them?
14. Are you using the gifts and talents that God gave you?
15. Are your relationships toxic? How do you handle them?
16. Do you have faith? How do you put it into action?

About the Author

Sharon Elvira Flowers was born on July 6, 1969, in E. St. Louis, Illinois to Johnnie L. McCray Sr. and Gladys L. McCray. She is the second of four children.

Dr. Flowers joined the US Army in 1988 and retired in 2008 after 20 years of faithful service to her Country.

In 2001, Dr. Flowers graduated with an undergraduate degree in Psychology and a minor in Sociology. In 2007 she graduated with her Master's in Education and a Doctorate in Psychology (2014).

Dr. Flowers was involved with *New Direction Church in South Carolina* working with a group named *Widows Connected* in which she would facilitate widows on how to move forward positively. She is currently serving with *Love Alive Church* in Orange Park, Florida as their Director of Education.

Dr. Flowers is presently preparing to present workshops at Fayetteville Technical Community College on Empowering Women, and she has previously presented a workshop on Posttraumatic Growth, Trauma, and Christian Spirituality.

The author is also working on another book, *Taken, But not Forsaken,* which focuses on the psychological struggles of trauma and healing using Biblical principles.

Dr. Flowers is married to retired (SGM) Nathaniel A. Flowers. Together the couple has eight wonderful children: Nathaniel

Jr., Felicia, Ni'Keysha, Fernandez, Steven, Dontel, Gabriela, and Kyndle.

You may contact the author via:

IG: @sharoneflowers,

FB: Sharon McCray Flowers,

Twitter: @DrSFlowers

Email: seflowers@icloud.com

Word Angels Books

an imprint of

Butterfly Typeface Publishing.

God's Word Lives On ...

Contact us for all your

publishing & writing needs!

Iris M Williams
PO Box 56193
Little Rock AR 72215

www.butterflytypeface.com

www.ingramcontent.com/pod-product-compliance
Lightning Source LLC
La Vergne TN
LVHW021504080426
835509LV00018B/2386